THE KEYS TO SUCCESS

by
JIM ROHN

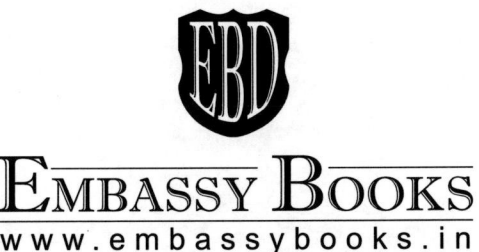

www.embassybooks.in

Published in India by :
EMBASSY BOOK DISTRIBUTORS,
120, Great Western Building,
Maharashtra Chamber of Commerce Lane,
Fort, Mumbai - 400 023. (India)
Tel : (022) 22819546 / 32967415
Email : info@embassybooks.in
Website : www.embassybooks.in

Cover design: Trish Hart
Typesetting: J A Crouch

Printed & Bound in India by Quarterfold Printabilities, Navi Mumbai

ISBN :   978-93-80227-77-1

CONTENTS

INTRODUCTION

Thirty years ago I was invited to share my experiences over a breakfast with a service group in Beverley Hills. Evidently the word spread and I was invited to speak to other service groups. Then a colleague asked me to address his marketing and sales team, and offered to pay me and I realised that people found something valuable in the experiences I was sharing. Since then, I have traveled the world in response to invitations to speak. I find my books on sale in many countries, and although I am primarily an entrepreneur, speaking to audiences is now a large and flourishing part of my business.

Although I still don't find being on stage comfortable, one of the greatest thrills of my life today is to get feedback from audiences and readers who have taken my story to heart, refined it for themselves and found something to enrich their health, their family life, their relationships or their businesses. I hope that through buying this book and reading it you might become one of the folk who gain value from what I have to say.

My commitment is to make the money you have spent, and the time you will spend on these pages, worthwhile. Especially the time. I have learned that you can always get more money but you can never get more time. But please don't gallop through from the first page to the last. Take notes, pause from time to time, put the book down, reflect. And if your life should change for the better because of this book, I would love to hear from you if ever our paths should cross.

Fundamentals

Let me begin by saying that I may write some things that are controversial. If I can provoke you to think, then I consider it worth it. No one person has all the truth. I don't claim to know it all, but I have found some answers. I have used them and they have been very beneficial in my personal and business life and that is what I want to share with you.

I don't expect you to follow everything I say, but I hope you take what makes sense, think about it, give it a try and refine it to suit yourself.

No one person has all the truth.

A Little About My Background

I was raised in a small village in Idaho, U.S.A. I graduated from High School and went to college for one year before quitting. I thought, foolishly, that I was smart enough. At age nineteen I got a job and thought, well, if I'm smart enough to get a job, surely that's smart enough. Then I met a beautiful young lady who was to become my wife, and I made all sorts of promises to her. She believed my grand promises about travelling the world, and wealth and fame and fortune, and so we were married. We began a family and little by little we began to fall behind.

I was working hard, but we were spending more than we were earning, and I was making no headway on my promises to my family. I had nothing invested for my future. The creditors were calling, and I was frustrated and broke and looking for some way to improve my life by the time I was twenty five. I thought about going back to school but that was a tough decision when I had a dependent family. And I had nothing with which to start a business.

Then good fortune came my way. I met a very rich man, a Mr. Earl Shoaff. A friend of mine worked for him and introduced me to him. Within a few minutes of meeting him I was dazzled. This man was wealthy but easy to talk to and I was impressed by his remarkable philosophy of life.

I thought then that the way to improve my lot was to get around someone like that and learn from him. My dream came true, Mr. Shoaff hired me and I was five years in his employ before he died at age fortynine. During this time he took the time to coach me and passed on the information about how he acquired his wealth and his good life.

I found out he had only been to the ninth grade. He never went to college but what he told me changed my life. It changed my finances. It changed everything. By the time I was thirtyone, I was a millionaire. Mr. Shoaff taught me economics, but even more valuable to me were the books he told me to read, and the changes he told me to make in my personality and language.

I will always be thankful to him for what he taught to me.

SET YOUR LIFE
ON THE COURSE
TO SUCCESS

CHAPTER ONE

WHAT I HOPE YOU WILL FIND IN READING THIS BOOK

1. Sincerity.

Mine and yours. You are obviously sincere to put your time and money into this book. But remember: sincerity is not a test of truth. Do not make the mistake of thinking, "He must be right, he is so sincere." It is possible to be sincerely wrong. The only test of truth is truth itself. I hope you will find what I write both sincere and truthful.

2. Ideas.

There is nothing so powerful as an idea whose time has come. In recent times we have witnessed how, when the walls of communism finally came tumbling down, there was no stopping democracy. In our lifetime we have seen this play out in history. An idea that comes at a good time can be so valuable. I hope you will find ideas here that will assist you in your personal, family and business decisions and I hope this is a good time for you. I don't know the timing of your life but this could indeed be a good time for you to set new goals and seek a new burst of life. It might just be a good time to look ahead and think about the type of person you want to be, the business you want to have and the bank balance you desire.

 There is nothing so powerful as an idea whose time has come.

3. Inspiration.

Inspiration is somewhat of a mystery. Who knows why some people are inspired and some are not? Some people have put up the money for this book while others have decided not to. Some are excited to be reading, others couldn't care less. These are what I call mysteries of the mind. There is a story that the day the Christian church was started, a great sermon was preached. It was preached to a multitude and there was a variety of reactions to the sermon. Some people were perplexed. Some laughed and mocked the speaker. Some who heard it had no idea what was going on. But some believed and the number was about three thousand. As far as we know, the preacher did not waste time trying to unperplex the perplexed, or to stop the mockers or enlighten those who didn't have a clue. There is a lesson in that you can't change people. I used to waste a lot of time trying to change people. But people can change themselves. All we can do is be a good example and dispense as much knowledge as we have and the rest is up to God and circumstances and the people themselves. What I have found is that if you share your experiences sincerely with someone they could be ready for change, but you really don't know.

 You can't change people,
but you can change yourself.

4. Guidelines.

Everyone can use a little coaching for their business life or family life or health. That is what I want to do - give a little coaching.

5. Translation.

The translation of my words into your life is up to you. I want you to get measurable results, but to do this you have to translate these guidelines into your personal situation - your income, your health, your family life, your bank account.

How To Get The Most Out Of This Book

1. Be thankful for what you already have.

Thanksgiving seems to open up the channels for receiving more. Cynicism stops the flow of good ideas but thankfulness for your education, freedom, democracy, culture, health, and opportunity will open you for more blessings.

2. Be eager to learn.

No matter what you have already learned, be eager to learn more. Sometimes, in the millionaires' club to which I belong, we have a billionaire come and talk to us because we always have more to learn.

3. Argue later.

I know I may be controversial, but my aim is to provoke

thought, not to give all the answers. The answers may be within you; I hope they are. But by listening to a variety of voices you can take the ideas and opinions of others and modify whichever of them you have to. Debate is vital to refining a good idea, and I challenge you to go over the ideas in this book with someone else. Ask yourself, "How do these ideas line up against my own experience?" Make sure whatever action you take then is the product of your own conclusion. Don't just act on what someone else says without debating and refining it for yourself. Of course, you may still make mistakes but you can always keep on refining. This is what I call fast-track learning: you take a concept, tease out the detail, refine it and apply it to your own experience.

4. Read with attention.

There is a world of activity going on outside the pages of this book and it is sometimes difficult to shut everything else - family, business, customers - out for a while. Zero in. Give these pages the best of your attention.

THE MAJOR KEYS TO SUCCESSFUL LIVING

Before I continue I wish to give an overview of the foundations I have referred to in my other books. My mentor, Mr. Shoaff, talked about "the halfdozen things that make eighty percent of the difference." For my purposes I have boiled that down to the Five Major Keys to Successful Living.

1. Philosophy.

This comes from using your mind to think to process ideas and information. This process establishes a guidance system, or a philosophy which will be a guidance system to get us through life emotionally, economically, spiritually and every other way. It is essential in order to avoid the dangers and take advantage of the opportunities. You need a good guidance system every time you step out the door. If your guidance system is imperfect you'll make colossal errors of judgement.

This system needs to be constantly refined. Philosophy is the major factor in how your life works out - what car you drive, where you live, what you wear, what you earn. I didn't used to think that. When I was twentyfive and broke I made a list of why my life wasn't going well. I blamed the government, taxes, negative relatives, unions, the weather. My mentor wouldn't accept my list of circumstantial causes. He told me the problem with my list was that I wasn't on it! I was waiting for a wind to blow me where I wanted to be.

We all need a wind to blow us to our dreams but there is not much you can do about the wind. We can't change it, but we can catch it. If you're waiting for a good wind to blow, you need to set your sails to make the most of it. That is what philosophy is all about: using your mind to think so that you can refine the set of your sails. The conversations you have with people you admire, the dialogue from good movies, song lyrics, sermons, literature and seminars can all help you constantly refine your guidance system and set a better sail.

 Set your sails to make the most of whatever wind may blow.

My mentor helped me set a better sail, and in the second six years of my economic life I went from being broke to being rich. Why? Not because the wind had changed but because I had set a better sail than from age nineteen to age twentyfive. All the other factors in my life were about the same but I had changed. I trust that the ideas in this book will help you set your sails to catch whatever wind may blow. We don't know which way the wind will blow but you can set a sail which will help you avoid the rocks where others will end up. While others are simply testing the wind, you can get busy on your self-education so that you can catch whatever wind there is to blow you to your dreams.

2. Attitude.

Have a good attitude about the past. Treat it as a school

or a teacher from whom you can learn. Don't let the past beat you, but teach you. Don't bear it like burden: if you carry it around like a great weight you will become too weary to make the most of opportunity. It will affect your health. You may have made mistakes but so have we all! This makes for experience and we can learn from that.

 Mistakes are the experience from which we can learn.

How you feel about the future is just as important. Have a good attitude looking to tomorrow. You need to have a destination in mind because if you don't know where you are going, how will you know when you get there? You won't know when to celebrate! Set goals. Surely every father would want a goal of financial independence for his family.

The future is promise.

This promise is an awesome force but you must be prepared to pay for the future with the present. Nothing is free. Everything has to be paid for. But remember, if the promise is clear, the price is easy. If you can see the promise of the future, the price is easy and you will be prepared to pay.

Have an educated attitude about everybody.

You can't succeed alone. It's hard to find a rich hermit! Each of us needs all of us. One person doesn't make a symphony orchestra or an enterprise or an economy. It takes all of us to create value, money, institutions that bless us all and so you have to learn to appreciate all of us. Learn to appreciate everybody's participation. Value everybody's gifts because they are necessary for an individual to be successful.

 Each of us needs all of us.

How you feel about yourself is important too.

Self esteem is the greatest step of progress toward success. You must develop self worth, self value. I believe that the greatest deterioration of self esteem comes through lack of simple disciplines. If you should do something, and you could do it, but you don't do it then that lack of discipline erodes self esteem.

It is easy not to do what we should. Self esteem begins to deteriorate when you do a little less than you can and then let yourself off the hook. It is the beginning of a slippery downhill slope. This is always a personal challenge: society does not care if you become financially independent or if you look after your health - you are the key. Society will not chastise you if you go soft on yourself, but neglect will destroy us all. Neglect will ace everyone and prevent us all from cashing in on opportunity. Neglect is like an infection that if not attended to will become a disease. One neglect leads to another like a domino effect. Neglect your economic situation and you'll soon neglect your health. Neglect your health and you'll probably neglect your friendships. Neglect your friendships and you'll probably find that soon you'll be neglecting your family.

But the simplest easy discipline returns self esteem. And each simple easy discipline also leads to another. Start eating an apple a day for your health and soon you'll also be taking a walk around the block. The simplest easy discipline rebuilds self esteem, turns it around and makes it positive. Long before you get a physical return from the discipline you will get increased self esteem.

 Self esteem is the greatest building block of success.

Begin the simple discipline of making a journal entry every day, and soon you will be making the time to read a paragraph from a new book. You will be paying more attention to the dialogue in a movie or a song. You will be more attentive to life. These simple things are the

12

first building blocks because all disciplines affect each other. Nothing stands alone. Everything matters. Some things matter more than others but there is nothing which doesn't matter.

*One lack of discipline
creates a character reaction.*

The good news is that each new discipline effects the rest, and leads to new ones. An apple a day can lead to other good health habits which can give you the energy to renew friendships and soon you are on an upward spiral. Whatever you do, don't let yourself off the hook.

3. Activity.

New life comes from labour - not from ideas and information alone. A great artist or architect may have ideas which are inspiring and show genius but unless they pick up a paintbrush or pencil there will be no painting or building. There is no business without activity - making phone calls, making sales, knocking on doors - no matter how wonderful the business plan. Without the labour there is no reality. You may have heard the phrase: No pain, no gain. Consider the mother who goes through labour pains to produce new life. If you wish to make a new life for yourself, you will need to labour. Affirmation alone will not do it. Affirmation without discipline is the beginning of delusion, but commitment to labour leads to the miracle of new life.

 **Wisdom uninvested in labour is wasted.**

This labour that works miracles is in two parts:

First, do what you can.

An ancient prophet said, "Whatever your hands find to do, do it." Don't neglect. If there's a call you must make, make it. If there's a conversation you must have, have it. Clean up all your neglect.

Ponder the question: "What am I not doing that would be easy to do? That would greatly affect my wealth and my health?" You are not asking here for the impossible. Just don't neglect what you can do. For example, if you wish to learn a language, commit yourself to three words a day. That equals one thousand words a year. This is easy to do, but also easy not to do. What is easy to do is always easy not to do. Remind yourself that you are not trying to do the impossible.

Second, do the best you can.

When I understood this aspect of labour, my income

multiplied miraculously. This is what brings visible results. My father gave me a seminar in one sentence: "Son," he said, "always do more than you get paid for, to make an investment in your future." Work on the principal: I should, I could and I will. If you should take a walk around the block and you could and you don't, that is the beginning of disaster.

Con Should, could, will: it will change your life. This is how you set your sail. You can handle complicated disciplines if you can handle small ones, so start with the small stuff first. How can you expect to clean up a corporation if you can't clean up your own garage? If you can be trusted with the easy disciplines, you will become a person who can be trusted with more complicated responsibilities, like running a corporation or handling a fortune. This principal applies to heath and relationships as well as to your finances, so practise the 'small stuff ' in all these areas before you move on to the bigger issues.

4. Results.

Philosophy plus attitude plus activity equals results. Results is the name of the game. That's why we read books like this and listen to tapes and go to seminars. That is why we practise the disciplines. In life we are presented with the seed and the soil and the seasons and the miracle of life, and life asks of us that we produce results. We have the opportunity: what can we do with it?

Look at your own results and then look around you

and learn from someone whose results are better than yours. Find someone who has done well and ask them if they will teach you from their experiences. Listen to them; take notes. That person might save you from a divorce if their marriage is happier than yours. They might save you from illness if they exude good health. Someone with healthy finances may be able to save you from bankruptcy, and a contented person may have something to say that would save you from heartache.

Learn from a successful person's experience to change your own results.

Life asks us to make measurable progress in reasonable time.

This is our challenge. Reasonable time may be twenty-four hours: you can measure how you are going at the end of each day. Don't let yourself off the hook. Remember, that a week of neglect in some circumstances may require a year of repair. For example, if you should have an important conversation with a child or a teenage son or daughter, you should have it today. In another week it may be too late. It's not worth it to let anything slide.

Sometimes, a reasonable time may be a week. A pay schedule for most people is one week. The company measures your performance each week and pays accordingly. I used to look at my pay packet and ask, "Is this all the company pays?" My mentor said, "No, Mr. Rohn, but that is all you are worth." What a revelation! I had to ask, what can I do to change my value? You can change your own value to your family or your company by measuring you own progress each week. Ask yourself for better results each week.

 Ask more of yourself.

5. Lifestyle.

For all of us, our philosophy, attitudes, and activity lead to results which in turn makes for lifestyle. Life style. I will refer to this in more detail later.

All of my seminars are drawn from the above five keys or foundations. I have devoted an entire book to them. They are the things which changed my own life the most.

SELF DEVELOPMENT
THE FIRST
STEP TOWARDS SUCCESS

CHAPTER TWO

PERSONAL DEVELOPMENT

The major challenge of life is to see what we can become - not to see what we can get. What we can become is what is important. The major question to ask of your job is, "What am I becoming here?" This is what is valuable - not what you can get out of your job, but what you can become through it. Mr. Shoaff said to me, "If you work hard on your job you can make a living. But if you work hard on yourself you can make a fortune." The key to all good is personal development.

 *Success is something that is attracted by self development.*

We are looking at economic success. Economics is the value you bring to the market place. This is what we get paid for. Sure, the market place takes our time but we do not get paid for that. We get paid for the value we

21

bring. I am not talking here about your value as a family member or a parent, or your value in the sight of God, but of market place value. The market place values some people at five dollars per hour, others at five hundred dollars per hour. There is a ladder of value and you must ask yourself the question, "How do I climb it?"

How do you climb it? How do you change your market value? Do you wait for a raise, or go on strike? Let me tell you, you can't get rich by demand. You get rich by performance. In this way you can increase your value by two, by five, by ten times. In the United States, there was a debate in Congress about raising the basic wage from five to six dollars per hour. I maintain that you don't need legislation to do that. It's such a small step on the ladder. Anyone can take that step by themselves.

Look up. See how far that ladder goes. You are supposed to climb it! There is plenty of room at the top: it's the bottom that is crowded! If you wish to increase your hourly rate, try whistling or smiling more while you work. Try improving your attitude, make yourself good to be around. It can lead to higher pay. When someone becomes valuable to the market place, the market place will pay them more. This is self evident. Evidently the person who gets paid a million dollars a year is more valuable to the market place than the one who gets paid a few thousand.

How high can you go on this ladder of value? How high does it go? You can go as high as you like, as high as you want to go. And here is the philosophy that will help you climb that ladder.

> *Work harder on yourself*
> *than on your job.*

You can do this step by step.

Start trying to be worth twice as much to your company: it will be embarrassing for them not to pay you more! Render service beyond what is required and you will be making an investment in your future that will bring incredible results. Even if you have a lousy job you can still increase your value. If you don't, you will always have the lousy job: you have to work on yourself before you can get a better job. The first six years of my working life I worked hard in my job and just made a living. The next six years I worked hard on myself and made a fortune.

Become more valuable to your family also. Skills are transferable: as you become more effective and skilful in the market place, you should become more effective and skilful at home. It would be tragic if you got better in the market place but not with your family. How could you inspire your employees but not inspire your children? It would be tragic too, if you had your sales people set goals but did not do it with your family. How could you treat your customers with respect but neglect your family? What an empty life that would be. An ancient prophet said of God, "His arm is not short." This should be true of every parent. You should be able to use your strengths to reach to everyone in your life. The greatest challenge in leadership is parenting. If you would be a good leader, be a good parent.

And more than that. President John Kennedy said, "Ask not what your country can do for you, but rather ask what you can do for your country." Ask yourself what you can do for your community, your country. What value can you bring? How can you help solve people's problems? Remember:

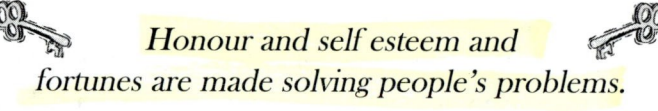

Honour and self esteem and fortunes are made solving people's problems.

If you think you are too busy to care about anybody else, then you will always be poor and pitiful. Self-care leads to poverty, self-investment leads to fortune. The fellow who arrives late, puts in a lazy day, takes a long lunch break and leaves early is sowing the seeds of his own disaster. He is becoming less than he could be. Render service beyond what is required because this is an investment that brings unbelievable results.

Don't look for a better job. The better job is looking for a better you. Work hard on making a better you. Work on your skills, your language, your vocabulary. Take classes, read books. Mr. Shoaff asked me how much of these things I was doing. I answered, "Zero." He shook his head. "Well, good luck," he said. He knew I would need it. He asked me how many books I had read in the last ninety days and how much money I had saved in the last six years. When I told him I had done nothing, he said, "Shouldn't we come and get your children and take them to safety!" I'm sharing with you what Mr. Shoaff shared with me because it changed my life.

CLIMBING THE LADDER OF OPPORTUNITY AT HOME AND AT WORK

Mr. Shoaff told me, "Mr. Rohn, you can have more than you've got, because you can become more." If you would have more the key is to go to work on yourself. Remember, it's not a matter of having more if they will pay more. No, they will pay more if you become more. Burn a little midnight oil in your quest to become more valuable.

 *Become more.*

Learn the lesson of the seasons.

The first thing to remember about the seasons if that you cannot change them. But the good news is that you can change yourself. If you want to know what the future will be like, look at the seasons and you'll see that it's going to be like it's always been - opportunity mixed with difficulty. It's been like that for the last six thousand years.

Sometimes there's more difficulty, sometimes there's more opportunity. I believe that at the moment there is more opportunity, and if we do it right as individuals, parents, businesses and leaders, we'll make everything ready for the twentyfirst century. If you will change, your income, you health, your skills will change and you'll become more attractive to the market place.

1. Learn how to handle the winters.

Winters come right after autumn, every year. It is not going to change! Some winters are longer and more severe than others but the cycle is the same. To think winter won't come is naive. The high flyers of the eighties thought it would be spring forever. That was foolish: to think there would never be another recession! These fellows cast all caution to the wind. They should have studied the history books and they would have learned that there will always be another winter.

There are all kinds of winters. There are economic, and political winters, such as the people of Eastern Europe suffered for so long. There are social and personal winters when your heart gets broken in a thousand pieces. You can't get rid of winter by tearing it off the calendar. But you can get stronger, wiser and better to deal with winters.

2. Learn how to take advantage of the spring.

Spring follows winter - how often? Every year for six thousand years! Wouldn't you agree these are good odds? These are the best you can get. Spring follows winter every time. Spring is opportunity and opportunity always follows difficulty. Expansion follows recession - every time.

Take advantage of it. Spring itself is a chance, not a guarantee, but that is all you need. You must plant in the spring, or you will beg in the autumn.

In the spring, you must hurry, because the window of opportunity doesn't stay open for ever. Farmers understand this. They don't take time off for sports and play in the spring because they know that the time for planting is limited. The window will close soon enough. Remember this, life itself is brief at the longest, so don't fool around. However many springs you have given to you, take advantage of them all. Whatever you do, don't just drift. Take advantage of every day, read every book you can read, learn every skill you can learn.

 The window of opportunity doesn't stay open forever.

3. In the summer you must nourish your values and fight your enemies.

As soon as you have planted the garden the weeds start to grow and become a threat. That's how life is. The bugs come out. So you must nourish your garden like a mother and defend it like a father. You can't ignore weeds. You need a hoe and some hostility to kill every weed you can kill if you want any garden left at all. The weeds will not go away if you just turn your head and play some kind of mind game. It's very important to love your values and hate your enemies. The ancient prophet said, "Love good and hate evil." "The things I once loved I now hate," he said, after his conversion.

You've got to be like your blood stream. You have red corpuscles to nourish and give life like a mother and white corpuscles to fight invasions and kill like a father. If your white corpuscles don't kill, the disease win kill you. You know with your own physical health that if you don't have a vigilant health plan with muscle, illness will muscle in.

When we went to war against Saddam Hussein some people questioned the value in fighting for a little country like Kuwait, but others saw that tyranny's appetite knows no restraint and that other countries in the Middle East and Mediterranean would soon be at stake. President Bush was right in drawing the line where he did. It is always better to draw the line early, rather than later. In your own life this is also true. Don't wait until the weeds have deep roots and long runners before you decide to act against them.

Some of your enemies are on the outside, some are on the inside. Beware of the thief in the alley after your purse, but what about the thief in your mind who wants to steal your promise? This thief tells you, You're too old, too short, too tired. This thief will try to talk you out of developing yourself and your skills. If you let him, this thief will render you weak and helpless. Worry alone will push you into a corner. Exercise your faith and conquer worry. You must not become a victim of yourself. As soon as you start any new project or relationship or company, it will have enemies and you will have to fight to maintain it.

4. In the harvest or autumn, reap without complaint.

Complaining is an illness that can become a terrible disease. This is your crop, so don't complain about it! You can change your income any time you want. You can take extra classes, or learn a new skill or go to the library, like others do to change their income. Don't tell yourself you can't do these things. You are not trapped in happy hour! Humans can use their minds to think and change their lives any time they want to; animals can't, but humans can. I tried to convince my mentor that it was external circumstances - the cost of things etc - but he wouldn't buy that. And once I understood that it was in me, not out there, I couldn't sleep nights. Start self education today put yourself on track for attracting good into your life. There is no better place to begin than here. Don't complain.

And don't apologise if you've done well. No complaint and no apology. What a place to arrive at, this place of maturity where you don't complain about your circumstances nor apologise for your success.

 *Take full responsibility for your harvest.*

THE THREE KEYS TO PERSONAL DEVELOPMENT

1. Physical.

You've got to like care of yourself. It's a major part of your future. An ancient scripture says, "Treat your body like a temple." What good advice. Treat your body like a temple, not a woodshed! Why? Because the body and the mind work together; one needs to be a support system to the other. You've heard the saying 'the spirit is willing but the flesh is weak.' What a tragic combination. The mind says, "Let's go get 'em," but the body can't get out of bed! Look at your body. Is it a good support system to your dreams? Talk to your body and train it to be full of energy to support your dreams; this is one of the most exciting disciplines in the world. Some people don't do well simply because they don't feel well.

> *Vitality plays an important role in success.*

Get smart, find out how to treat your body well. Study nutrition. My mother knew about nutrition, and even though she was born with a very fragile heart, she was 78 before she had a heart attack and she recovered from that. A second heart attack took her away but the doctor said that through good nutrition she had extended her life by at least fifteen years. As a result of her care, example and the knowledge she passed on, my Poppa and myself and my own children have never had a day's illness. Take care of your body. Some people take more care of their animal's diet and exercise programme than they do of themself.

When you start feeling vitally strong and healthy there is no telling what you can do! It doesn't take more than a few minutes a day to begin taking some exercise? A daily walk around the block is not a difficult thing to schedule in.

In exercising, be conscious of self, but not self conscious. You don't need an eight hour a day muscle building programme! Forty-five minutes a day will keep you healthy. Take the stairs instead of the escalators. Eat fruit. Little things every day will improve your health.

Take care of your appearance too.

How we get valued in the market place is also dependent on how we look. God looks on the inside, but people look on the outside. You may say that people shouldn't judge you by appearance, but they do! Make sure the outside is a good indication or reflection of the inside.

2. Spiritual.

This is my opinion, but I get paid big money to share it, so I tell you that I think this is the important side. Some people believe that humans are just advanced animals, but I wonder how words like love and honour and justice fit into an animal's vocabulary! They just don't mean anything to a crocodile, even an advanced one! But what you believe is up to you. My suggestion is that if you believe in the spiritual life, do not neglect the study and the practise of it.

 Honour your spiritual side.

3. Mental.

We need mental food to nourish the mind. Books and seminars provide food for thought but some people read so little they've got rickets of the mind. What good are fantastic muscles in your body if you are weak in the mind? Some folk can't defend an argument or fight for their family's future because they haven't built mental muscles. It's not the body but the mind which will work out the miracle of your future, so don't shortchange it.

 Don't neglect to feed the mind.

An ancient prophet said that humans cannot live just on bread. Animals can, but not humans: we also need words that become food for the mind. Learn to have an appetite for words. Learn to appreciate songs and screenplays and sermons because we nourish the mind with words in order to see. The ancient prophet also said that words are like a lamp for your feet, and like a light for your pathway. Without them you will not know where to go in your life. Words are so important as illuminating light! Words develop concepts and formulate philosophy. This is where we differ from animals.

You will need a library of your own to provide food for the mind. A personal development library must be well balanced. You cannot live on mental candy or mental ice-cream. Some people say they just read that positive stuff, but it's not enough. In life you need to be negative as well. You've got to have the ant philosophy: ants think winter all summer. It's easy to get fooled by blue sky and warm weather but you need to think about storms and rain. You've got to think of the negatives when everything is positive. Ants also think summer all winter you also have to think positive when everything seems negative. After all, how long can winter last? So, with regard to your library, learn from the ants. Remember too that ants never quit, even when someone tries to stop them. They just find another way. And they gather as much as they possibly can when there is food to gather. It's a simple lesson that makes for safety and joy. Why would you settle for anything less anyway?

Gather as much as you can - learn as many skills, and develop your talents and make as many friends as you can and travel as much as you can and share as much as you can. If you do just enough to get by in all these things, you will not create happiness for yourself. All life forms strive to their maximum potential except, it seems, human beings! How tall will a tree grow? As tall as it possibly can! Trees don't grow to half their height and then stop. Why don't human beings realise their full potential? Because we have been given the dignity of choice. We are not just driven by instinct and our genetic code. This dignity of choice is to become part of what we can become or to become all that we can possibly become. I ask you to consider becoming all that you can possibly become: the best father, the best mother, the best citizen, the best worker. Stretch yourself to your full potential. Live life to the max. Be a student of the ants!

 Become the best you possibly can.

You need to read autobiography and biography. Read stories of unique people. Study society by all means, but read the story of outstanding individuals. In this study you need contrast - Hitler and Gandhi. One to show you how high the human spirit can go, and the opposite to show you how low. The stories of people in the Bible show both sides of human nature.

Read about good health. This will permeate not just you but your children and their children too. It will be part of your legacy.

Also read good novels. Sometimes an author is brilliant at teaching philosophy through an absorbing story. But skip the trash. You might find a crust of bread in the garbage, but is it worth it? You don't need to do that!

Study law.

You don't need to be a lawyer, but you need to know how to read the fine print. You need to know what to sign and what not to sign. Know about contracts. Know what a handshake means. Learn enough law to keep yourself straight and out of trouble. I was a millionaire at thirty-one, but I was broke at thirty-three. Mr. Shoaff died and I lost his influence, and I set about trying to buy the world and I made some foolish business decisions. I guaranteed to back a company without reading the fine print, and although I thought I was committed to one instance, in fact I had signed a continuing guarantee and as a result I lost a great deal of money. I knew the company was going bad and would never have become involved in guaranteeing their second loan, but it was too late. I received the demand in the mail and I was legally responsible. You need to be aware of these things!

Understand basic accounting.

To do this you will need to read up on it. You will need to know how to keep track of your resources.

Be a student of culture.

Study the fine things that appeal to the high side of your nature. We must be better than civilised, we must be refined. Make a contribution to your country by becoming sophisticated, not just civilised. Learn what true values are. There is no substitute for reading books. If your library includes food for thought from a variety of sources you will become self-educated. Keep the learning curve high and you will be glad you did.

DEVELOP THE ABILITIES ESSENTIAL FOR SUCCESS

CHAPTER THREE

UNDERSTANDING SUCCESS

Four Steps To Success

As you work on your self-development, the following four things will form steps to your success.

1. Be a student of good ideas.

Learn to log them and keep a journal of good ideas. Don't trust your memory. If you find a good health idea - jot it down. When you hear a good business idea - write it down. Journals are for serious students. In every area of your life, you should have journals where you have listed new, good ideas which form the guidelines of your life. Be this serious about your future.

2. Have good plans.

Plans are putting your good ideas to work to make dreams come true. You need a good health plan. You need a good financial plan. Don't let yourself slide on developing good strategies, tactics, concepts and details. Keep adding refinement and experience to your bank of knowledge and keep finding ways to make your ideas work. This is how you build up equities of the mind and the treasures of the heart, the soul, the spirit such as health and a good marriage and friendships. Collect ideas for your plans and then execute them.

3. Learn to handle the passing of time.

There are two things that will destroy you quicker than anything - greed and impatience. You must learn to be patient. You have to give your project time. It takes time to build a corporate career or a strong family. It takes time to put together a symphony orchestra that plays the music that inspires everybody. Give yourself time too! Don't set a ninety-day time limit on learning something new, don't be impatient. What if kids gave up on learning to tie their shoes!

Greed is a deadly disease. Contrary to what the movie *Wall Street* suggests, greed is not good. It's evil and we must legislate against it. We have seen greed in the early nineties and eighties. Greed hopes for more than its share, something for nothing, something at the expense of others and this is evil. Legitimate ambition is something else altogether and that is good: gaining a fortune at the service, rather than at the expense of others, gaining by making products or services more valuable. If you help enough people get what they want you can have all you want, as Zig Ziglar says, "Greed is not necessary in order to become wealthy."

> *Learn to invest in yourself and in other people and you can become wealthy without greed.*

The American push-button society is so impatient it is out of control. People get worked up if nothing happens in two seconds. It's fun to watch Americans in Spain which is somewhere else all together! The Spanish have practised waiting! It drives Americans crazy. I see impatience on the road all the time. People will betray themselves rather than wait two or three seconds. Patience means you will hang in there when others leave.

4. Learn to solve problems.

Life is solving a set of problems! Neil Armstrong said that going to the moon and back was simply solving two problems - how to get there and how to get back. He said the secret was not to leave before both problems were solved. In business, you need to solve the problem of going into a project, but also how to get out of it.

Write you problems down on one side of a sheet of paper. This will help you analyse them. Some people might think this is negative, but you need to do this. This isn't the same as dwelling on your problems, even if you write out all that's bad, because solutions will suggest themselves in the act of writing down on paper. Leave the right hand side of the paper for the answers to your challenges.

I have found that there are three questions that will help solve any set of problems.

First, ask "What could I do?"

When looking at your problems, search your mind for possibilities and options for things to do. List your alternatives and evaluate them - "This would take too long" "This would cost too much" - in writing, on the page. Unless you are an absolute genius you will need these working papers where you take material out of your head and set it down in front of you.

Your first answer to this question might be, "I don't know what I could do." That's okay.

Ask yourself the next question, "What could I read?" because a book might contain the results of someone else's research into your problem. A couple of days' reading can give you access to a lifetime of someone else's hard work.

*There is no substitute
for reading books.*

Don't leave the reading until too late. A friend of mine lost one of the most wonderful women I have ever known, and the tragedy was that later, he found in his own library, a book that might have saved his marriage!

If you have read several books and still haven't found the answer, ask yourself the third question. "Who can I ask?"

You should not hesitate to ask for help, but don't ask first. See if you can solve the problem yourself first, to develop your own mental muscle. Remember that practise is as valuable as an answer. You need the practise! In sales we say, practise is as good as a sale. It helps you develop the skill, not just the answer, an answer is temporary but a skill is permanent. Keep going until you develop the skill. When you ask someone, and you show the person that you have already been through your working papers, they will give you good advice because they will see that first you were willing to help yourself. They will know that their advice will not be wasted.

There are times when it is legitimate to ask, "Will you help me," but a better question is, "Will you teach me?" If you try your best to get some answers and don't go for shortcuts, you will get them. People are more than willing to teach, to invest time in, someone who shows they are willing to invest in themselves.

CONDUCT IN THE MARKET PLACE

Another aspect of self development concerns how we conduct ourselves in the market place. Find out as much as you can about your own job, where you work and your industry, it's not enough just to have the appropriate skills, you need to be aware of your conduct as well as your skill. You don't want to lose chunks from your potential pay packet through behaviour which might be acceptable somewhere else but not in your corner of the market place.

 We should all be students of the market place.

Language

Be careful of your language in the market place. This could be very costly to you and your future. Bad language may be costing you thousands per year. This is not a moral question, this is simply a question of consequences. Some stories may be suitable for the bar but not for the market place, but good language is acceptable anywhere!

Habits

In your own corner of the market place this may also be important. Casualness may lead to casualty! Smoking may be a habit that costs you in your market place. Tardiness may cost you dearly and if you added up a decade of being late, you might discover that it has cost you more than you wanted to pay! I'm not asking you to be anything you are not, or to sell out yourself, but just to be aware of what your habits may be costing you. Be careful.

Dress

Dress is another thing that you need to be conscious of in the market place. Save your open shirt and gold belt and your pointed yellow shoes for the disco! Different corners of the market place, different localities, have different dress standards and if you are a student of the market place you will understand this.

Only bring your skill to the market place, not your need

The market place doesn't want to know your need. Bring your eagerness, not your need. When applying for jobs this will be important - your preparedness to do more may gain you employment ahead of others who are most concerned to make sure their own needs are being met. Don't talk about your illnesses or money or relationship worries at work or in the market place. It is too costly. The market place is the soil and will only provide you with a crop if you bring your seed to it, not your need.

In all this, be open to getting some help

Ask someone who has your interests at heart for advice and feedback on how you are going in all these aspects. Be prepared to hear the truth. You may be unaware of how you are behaving, because some habits are almost unconscious. Often people will not tell you what you really need to know about your habits, because it is so sensitive. But if you invite them to tell you, you open the door to receiving good advice. Listen to the feedback because to ignore it may cost you dearly. This is part of your education, your grooming for success.

In my own experience this works. I have had to take advice on material in my seminars, even though at first I was defensive and would justify it. My friend suggested I think over some aspect of my presentation and I resisted it for a day or two but then I realised he was right. The words I was using would have cost me more than they were worth to leave them in.

I had to take advice on dress. I had to be told that white socks did not go with a black tuxedo. I was, after all, a farm boy from Idaho. You might need that kind of advice. You might need someone to let you know how you are going with your language and your habits.

Perhaps you need feedback too, on how you look or how you smell.

You can listen or not listen. You might decide to act and dress however you want. But I am simply saying that if you are working on your self-development, this kind of study of the market place is another aspect of it.

THE FIVE ABILITIES

In my experience, I have found that the following five abilities are an essential aspect of self-development.

1. Develop the ability to absorb.

Absorb each day. Treasure it as a piece of the mosaic of your life. Think about each day, store occasions away in your memory bank. Don't just try to get through the day, get from it. Let the drama of the day soak into your consciousness. Remember the occasion as much as the notes you take from a meeting or seminar. Absorb the people and their energy not just their ideas. Treasure the sights and sounds and smells and flavours. Let life have its impact on you.

 Observe and absorb.

2. Develop the ability to emotionally respond.

Learn to be affected. Don't just respond with talk Capture each day in your spirit and respond deeply to it. Let sad things make you sad, let tragedy make you cry, let happy things make you happy. Let your emotions respond to life. The key is this: let life touch you, not kill you. Learn to let life stir you, not just provide you with intellectual stimulation. At a movie, for example, let yourself be provoked and swept up by the drama and the music and the dialogue. Learning to respond like this will create a bank of richness inside you to draw from.

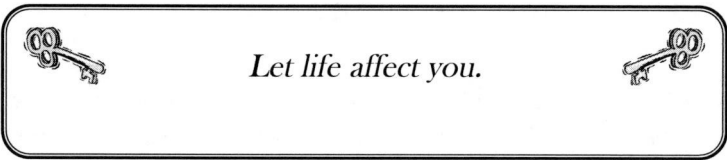

Let life affect you.

3. Develop the ability to reflect.

It makes the past more valuable. Take the time to go back over it. Run the tapes again of your intellectual and emotional experiences. Take a few moments to go over the day at the end of it, to lock it in. What went right and what went wrong today? How did you feel? Use your journal to record it all.

At the end of the week, take a few hours to go over everything you have done during the past seven days. Lock it in. And at the end of the month, take half a day to go back over everything. At the end of a year, take a weekend to contemplate the last three hundred and sixty-five days of your life. In the Old Testament they had sabbaticals - one year to go over the previous six years. Not just for rest but to consider what had happened. In the New Testament it talks about taking the time to go into a closet and shut yourself away.

Someone asked me if I meditate. I said, "I don't know but I certainly mull." It is so valuable to ponder and wonder about life. You might do this by shutting yourself away or by going out into the outdoors. This is how you make the past valuable. When you understand its value that it is coin, currency you can invest it in your future. Don't waste it. Take the treasure of the past and invest it in your future, so that you can make the next six years three or four or five times more valuable than the last six. Some of the biggest fortunes are not made until after age sixty-five because there are so many years, so much treasure invested.

 Take the treasure of the past *and invest it in your future.*

4. Develop the ability to act.

Don't waste your first three abilities by not ever acting on them! What is the point of having seed corn you never plant, or an account on which you never draw. You write a cheque on the past through action for the future.

Treasures of friendship, income, personal relationships and good health will flow back to you in abundance.

 *Put your abilities to work.*

5. Develop the ability share.

Affect someone else. Let me tell you that there is no greater experience. Invest life into life and it will work miracles. Pass on what you know. Share poems, books, disciplines, recipes with others. Practise the art of sharing by first sharing every little thing, and then life will give you something big to share. I started out by sharing with one, then two, then three people. Now I speak to millions. When I started motivating I was already making a fortune so I was willing to give my knowledge away, to share it for free. And then someone offered to pay me. But I get so excited doing seminars that I wouldn't miss them for anything. I get to hear this good stuff over and over again.

When you share, everybody wins. The person who shares may win more than the person who receives. At one of my seminars a lady asked me how I managed to stay excited all the time. I told her that one of the reasons was that when I shared my excitement, I always got excited!

A full glass will hold more only if you pour some out first. That is what I am asking you to do. You cannot hold more until you pour out for others - heart, soul experiences. Unlike a glass which stays the same size, with human beings, the more you pour out, the more you grow, and the more you can give out again. Don't hold back, don't turn your glass upside down. There is plenty in this life to share and if you are miserly with what you have, it's like going to the ocean with a teaspoon.

Over the years I have given away thousands of copies of a book called *The Richest Man in Babylon*. I don't begrudge it because I know there is no telling what effect that book can have. I get feedback from people who have attended my seminars ten or twenty years ago and it is enormously gratifying to hear of their success. A coach feels fantastic when one of their students becomes a star. When Tony Robbins was seventeen he attended one of my seminars and he became immediately intrigued with what he heard. He came to work for me and after three years he was running one of my offices. Of course, now he has mastered these studies and become a superstar with his own programmes, and that is exciting for me.

I'm asking you to affect someone's life. You never know when what you share will change someone's life in health or family relationships or finances. You can start a chain reaction and you never know where it will end. It may do wonders for someone else, but it will also do wonders for you.

 The more you give out the more you grow.

LIFESTYLE

In the first chapter I wrote about The Major Keys to Successful Living: philosophy, attitude, activity, results, and lifestyle. I will devote a few pages to lifestyle here because lifestyle is the ultimate challenge of life.

I believe that what constitutes a good life is balance. Take the results of your philosophy, attitude and activity and fashion for yourself a good life. Like weaving a tapestry. You can't just leave it to happen. It won't, you have to work at it yourself.

The four parts of a good life

1. Pleasure.

You can't know pleasure unless you're educated. Good taste is an education. There is a difference between cola and fine wine. You cannot know the pleasure of a symphony or a painting or poem unless you have been educated. So make sure you become educated for lifestyle, not just commerce. Persist in your studies of taste and culture, of poetry and art and sculpture.

A wine connoisseur once told me he rated Bulgarian wines low because they came on too strong and were too bold, but after he had been to Bulgaria and met the people and walked their fields and villages he realised that no wine in the world better represented the people who made it. He educated himself and thereafter took intense pleasure in Bulgarian wines.

 Good taste is an education.

2. Happiness.

Happiness doesn't just blow in your window. You have to educate yourself for it. The American Constitution states that the pursuit of happiness is basic to life. It recognises that happiness does not happen by chance, it is something you have to go after.

To create happiness you have to study it. I have learned that happiness is an art: it needs to be fashioned and designed. Even such a simple thing as a "happy birthday" has to be designed, or the day may not be happy at all. You can become a genius at creating happy occasions, or lifestyle, in your own home. I guarantee that when you think of ways to make others happy, it will make you happy. Money has little to do with it. Wealthy people have to fashion their happiness the same as anybody else. What a tragedy when a man studies economics but neglects to study lifestyle. How sad for a parent to throw money at a child and expect the relationship to reward him/her with happiness.

Happiness is an art study it!

From my mentor I learned a lesson in creating moments of happiness. Mr. Shoaff taught me that "tips" had another meaning apart from dollars and cents. T.I.P.S. = To Ensure Prompt Service! He taught me that the way to ensure an excellent dining experience was to pay the tip up front, before the meal. He said, sophisticated people do not take a chance on good service. He would take a waiter aside before the meal and offer ten dollars when asking the man to look after himself and his friend throughout the meal; the waiter was invariably happy, and Mr. Shoaff always had a good meal.

 *Create joy.*

3. Joy.

You can create your own joy. Some occasions are so wonderful you cannot even give them language. Joy is indescribable, but it is an essential part of lifestyle.

4. Ecstasy

In creating lifestyle, you will create moments of ecstasy We call them moments because they do not last forever.

Friends, lovers, family can bring you moments of ecstasy but you have to put yourself out to get the rewards. They do not come while you're sitting at home on the couch.

Nature can provide you with such moments. Trout fishing at dawn can reward you with unbelievable moments of ecstasy but you have to get up early and drive when others are still sleeping and wade into cold water and sit in your old boat in darkness until the sun comes up and the fish leaps on your line. No words can describe the thrill, the ecstasy of fighting that trout on the line and landing it as the sun comes up to shine on its black back and coloured belly.

I'm asking you to find ways to live well. Don't miss out on extraordinary events by not bothering to put yourself out. I missed an opportunity to hear Barbra Streisand sing at a concert for the first time in twenty years because I did not take the opportunity. Those who were there spoke of moments of ecstasy. Tell yourself, "I am going to learn to design a life, not just live!" Don't say no to an opportunity to live. Don't put things off; put yourself out. I missed seeing Louis Armstrong perform live because I did not make the effort and take the time. Opportunities for refined pleasure pass if you do not take them when they present themselves.

Design life
- don't just live it.

ENLIGHTENED SELF INTEREST

This is one of the most important studies in personal development that I ever undertook. The first question that I had to ask was, "Is it moral, is it legitimate to act in my own self interest?" When I finally came to the conclusion that it was okay to act in my own self interest that was a great discovery for me.

Enlightened self interest is different from selfishness. Selfishness is like greed, hoping for something at the expense of others, wanting more than your share, but enlightened self interest is built within all of us. Is it okay to be interested in ourselves? My studies revealed that yes, it is okay if everybody wins. That added incredible dimensions to my life. If you win at the expense of others that's not okay, but if you win by contributing to others that sort of self interest is okay.

There are enlightened ways to act in your own self interest, and I call these success equations. They are so simple that children can learn them

Jesus said that if you wish to be the greatest you must find a way to serve the many. Now, I am no authority on the Bible, but the fact that he said it at all indicates to me that it is okay to wish for such a thing; but it is the second half of the sentence that is so revealing. I've restated it to read like this: service to many leads to greatness. Great wealth, great respect, great treasure, great trophies, great fortune, great feeling.

All kinds of greatness comes from service to many.

This is the secret to enlightened self-interest. This equation means that everybody wins, nobody is left out.

Jesus also said that if you wish to be a ruler over much (whether a city, a fortune, or great treasure) then you must be faithful when the amounts are small. Again, there is an equation here and it is the second half that is interesting. I've translated the "be faithful" into "be disciplined." Be disciplined when the amounts are few and then you can be ruler when the amounts are many. What a colossal awareness and understanding!

Some people foolishly say that if they had a fortune they would take care of it. They complain, "But I only have a pay cheque so I don't know where it goes." If you can't be wise with your pay check, who would entrust a fortune to you? If you despise your little job and goof off, you'll never be trusted with an important job. Have you ever said, "I don't know where it all goes. It just gets away from me!"? Who would trust you to run a company or to run the world?

 The time to qualify for leadership
is when the amounts are small.

Ancient Scripture asks, "Should we give a man a city to run if he can't preside over himself?" Over his own appetites, himself. It's called self control. If you take care of the small things in your charge, you will qualify for bigger responsibilities.

Life operates to give us what we deserve, not what we need.

That was a revelation to me. Once I understood that, I could act in my own self interest in an enlightened way. The great law of the universe does not read: If you need, you will reap. No, it reads: If you plant, you will reap. If you need to reap, then you need to plant. Life was designed to respond to the planters, not the needers.

If you search you will find.

Note that finding is reserved for those who deserve it. Who deserves to find? Those who search! If you wish to find in your own self interest, you have to become a searcher. Search for truth. For good ideas you have to go search in the library, the class, the book, in church, at the seminar. Rarely does a good idea interrupt you on its own. But there are plenty of good ideas for those who look for them.

If you wish to receive, you must give.

Wishing to receive sounds like self interest. But when you are enlightened you know that you must first give. Those who don't know better think that if you give, it's gone. No. That's ignorance. If you give, it's invested. What do we expect from an investment? A return, multiplied! If you give, everybody wins because you also get a return with interest. Isn't that extraordinary!

It's much better to give than to receive.

For the uneducated that doesn't make sense. That is why John Kennedy said, "Ask not what the country can do for you, but what you can do for your country." That's not operating in your own self interest. It's better to give than receive because giving starts the receiving process.

You must always pay fair price.

Truly sophisticated people will always say "I wish to pay fair price, for what it makes of me to pay it." This is a startling equation. The paying will make something of the person. The uneducated person wants things for nothing, or they want them cheap. If you get something for nothing, you can be nothing. If you want it cheap, you can be cheap. But that's not where the joy and dignity is. Tell yourself, "I wish to be someone of value and so I will pay a fair price." Paying makes something of your character, your skill, your time, your substance. Learn to give for what it makes of you as a person.

DEVELOP THE ART OF GOOD COMMUNICATION

CHAPTER FOUR

COMMUNICATION

For good communication you have to have an understanding of words. Understand that words are almost
Godlike in power. Earlier we said they were like bread,
too. The power of words is extraordinary and that is why
you must be a student of them. Nothing is richer than
the English language. We have words to persuade,
inspire, instruct and to paint the promise of the future.

One ancient prophet said, "The word was God. And
God was the word." I take this to mean that words are
almost Godlike in power. The Bible story of creation is
unique: it talks about words creating light. How often
have people said, "I was in the dark but now I see"? Or,
"While you were talking, it dawned on me"?

I'm asking you to not be lazy in conversation, and
become a diligent student of words. Words are so
powerful in framing ideas. In my country, the founding
fathers put together the Declaration of Independence,

which was an act of treason. They needed a powerful document to express their format for a new nation. When the document was finished they said, "To this idea we now pledge our lives and our fortunes and our sacred honour." What an example of the power of words!

The possibilities of language are electrifying. For your future, for your family, for your fortune. Words can motivate someone to change their ways, to go over their mistakes, to walk out of the ghetto. I met a man who only went to the ninth grade but he was gifted in language in a simple way. He told me I had "messed up". But he didn't leave me with those words. He added words that inspired me to change my life. His words kept me from sleeping nights. In your family, what you say is so important. In management, in sales and business there is no more powerful tool.

 *Know the power of words.*

Communication is affecting other people with words. This is what I have laboured for thirty four years. I want my words to create life and sight, to develop answers, to provoke, portray, illuminate. I want my readers and students to see nuances, shades of meaning and possibilities. And over the years I have found that there are four steps that lead to communication.

1. Have Something Good To Say.

That's obvious, isn't it. But success is a refined study of the obvious; if you brush up on the obvious you can start going for your fortune! Now, there are a number of factors in having something good to say. First you must be prepared. And to prepare well you need to prepare with purpose and prepare on purpose. A strong enough purpose - to make a sales career, to become an entrepreneur, to develop your family's promise for the future - will drive you to prepare properly, and proper preparation means you are deliberate and consistent in your studies.

 Communication needs to be a daily practise.

Preparation takes time. We are not like a wildebeest which must walk within a few minutes of being born, and which can run with the herd an hour later. Humans take time to prepare; the sad thing is that many are not ready after seventeen or more years.

Preparation means that you will have a verbal cheque to cash when you get ready to talk. You can't draw on an account that doesn't exist, on experience you haven't had or preparation that you've never made. If you prepare yourself, you will have something to draw on when you talk. And if you speak only what is the tip of the iceberg of what you have prepared, then you will communicate well. People will get the feeling that if you had to you could talk for an hour, that you have a hundred illustrations. You don't need to use all your preparation, but people will get the sense that you have a wealth to draw on.

Be interested in life and people.

Study people and find out what makes them tick. Study their backgrounds, their mannerisms, their temperaments. Be a student of business life and political life, of people and systems. Read the newspaper and magazines; be interested in the whole world, not just your corner of it. Be able to continually debate the major life issues and political conflicts. You will be able to contribute to debate at work and in your family if you are informed and interested. To be a good communicator you have to keep up with current events. Locally, know what is happening at your school. What are they teaching the kids? What political side are they leaning to? When I started speaking in some schools teachers were suspicious of speaking about capitalism, and that was in a capitalist society! They couldn't yet see that capital belonged in the hands of their students. What is going on your area? Stay in touch, be interested.

 Be a student of life.

Be fascinated.

Fascination goes beyond interest. Interested people ask, "Does it work?" but fascinated people ask "How does it work?" Ask questions that go deeper than surface examination. Children have the unique, childish quality of fascination and that's why they learn so much in their first seven years. Learn to be fascinated with what you see, hear and read. Have the attitude that you have to know! Ask, "What makes people act like that?" "How come I react like this?" This kind of curiosity, this desire to know, will bring you incredible learning.

Turn frustration into fascination: you'll learn more. When you are stuck on the freeway, and you've got a plane to catch, don't be frustrated, be fascinated. Of course, it doesn't work every time, but you will get more from that life experience if you get fascinated, not frustrated. You can even get fascinated with your own frustration. I used to get frustrated with the Bible, but now I let it fascinate me. There are things I didn't used to understand; now I learn from them. The story of Job is one example. It starts with a scene where God and Satan are talking, and Satan offers God a deal to test Job's faithfulness. Satan bets that Job will curse God when Satan is allowed to get at him. Satan begins by taking his family, then his wealth, then his health. Job ends up sitting in the ashes scraping at his sores with a rock, but despite his wife's attempts to get him to curse God, he doesn't. God wins the bet. And then he makes everything up to Job and doubles his blessings. This story fascinates me, even though I'm not sure I understand it.

Be sensitive.

You have to be sensitive to people and where they find themselves at the moment. Be sensitive to people who are not like you. If you are poor you have to be sensitive to the rich, and the rich must be sensitive to the poor. Be sensitive to other people's tragedies.

I've had to work on this because I have never had tragedy in my life. I was an only child, spoiled, and I found a mentor at age twenty-three who helped me become wealthy. I made myself go to San Francisco and spend time on the street of lost souls to learn about tragedy. Of course, you can't really know what it's like unless you've lived it, but you can try. This will help you communicate better.

There's truth in the old saying, "You can't understand a person until you've walked in their shoes." When I was spending time in the Tenderloin, the lost souls area of San Francisco, I talked to a bartender who showed me more tragedy in a week than most people see in lifetime. He told me all the tragic stories of the people in his bar. I learned so much from him and it softened the bluntness of my communication. If you are sensitive, you will find more compassion than contempt when you stand up to speak.

 Compassion opens closed doors.

Be knowledgeable.

You also have to be knowledgeable if you want to have something good to say. Keep learning, keep listening, keep attending classes. Spend a part of your income on continuing self education. A manufacturer puts aside finance to replace old machinery with new; you have to do the same, with your knowledge and ideas.

Now, with regard to good communication, there are four "keys" that make life worthwhile.

i. Life is worthwhile if you keep learning.

Never cease your quest for knowledge. Learn the systems and the equations and the possibilities as well as the dangers and pitfalls.

ii. Life is worthwhile if you try.

Put your hand to it. Give your education a chance to function. And don't just try once; keep on ... until! How long should a baby try to walk? The answer is... until! You don't know how high you can jump or how far you can possibly run unless you keep going ... until. You don't know if you've got what it takes until you do it.

iii. Life is worthwhile if you stay.

Some people don't hang around to see the seasons through Some people spend their life building foundations but never staying long enough to put up the walls and the roof. See things through. If you sign up to play

73

the game, see it through to the finish. Practise this anywhere. If you buy a ticket to a game, stay until the end. It's not good for morale if the spectators leave before the game is over!

A great Christian leader wrote, knowing that the end was near, "I fought a good fight." Fight for your family, your health, your business.

He also said, "I finished the course." He got his work done. He didn't give up, and neither should you.

"I kept the faith," he added. That's an important reputation to earn. Keep faith with your family, your ideology, your beliefs.

Finally the leader said, "I'm ready for the crown." He knew he had deserved the prize, the reward.

iv. Life is worthwhile if you care.

If you care at all you get some results, if you care enough, you can get incredible results.

The next step to good communication is:

2. Say It Well.

If you have all the knowledge but you can't deliver it well, no one will understand you.

The first important aspect of saying it well, is sincerity. You also need the repetition of practise. You have to practise your delivery in all fields of communication whether you are talking to your customers or your children. At first I was nervous to speak in public, but I didn't let my fear stop me and now, after a few thousand speeches, I can speak without notes for hours. Your practise must be with purpose though. You practise in order to get better, sharper, more effective. By practicing you will learn to choose the right words for your delivery. Mistakes in language, remember, can cost you too much. You might stutter or hesitate or choose a clumsy expression when you start, but through the repetition of practise it doesn't matter if it takes years - you will get better.

And in all your communicating brevity is important. Sometimes the more brief the communication, the more pointed. Don't go on and on. Children will teach you this: after thirty seconds they are wondering just how long you are going to take! Jesus was a master of this. To some, all he had to say was "Follow me." How could he be so brief? Because of who he was. His reputation preceded him, so that when he got there, he didn't have to say much. That's why we focus on personal development: if you get the right reputation, you may not need many words.

To speak well you have to have style. Of course, your style may well depend on your background - in Italy everyone talks with their hands! Be a student of effective style but don't just copy someone. Watch other speakers' gestures, expressions and blend what you learn to make it yours. Have your own style. I have picked up things from other speakers, and have been influenced by them, but I have not copied them.

In sales training we teach that the manner is more

important than the matter. You don't want poor style to get in the way of good information, and it may be helpful to have a little coaching in this area. We all remember teachers who entertained us with their style. And we took in the information because they were real in their enthusiasm and their gestures and expressions fascinated us.

It's not so much what you say but how you say it.

Have a good working vocabulary. A study among prisoners revealed that there is definitely a relationship between vocabulary and behaviour. Why? Vocabulary is a way of seeing. You can't change the picture in your mind if you have limited words: you are like a painter with a limited colour palette. We can only see the problem or the answer or experience with our present vocabulary. In the interest of your own exciting future, get yourself a vocabulary that translates well so that you will be able to translate the beauty and the poetry and the symmetry of life.

If you have a small vocabulary, you have a small world. You are looking at life through a small hole. Get a dictionary to add to your library, and keep adding words to your life. Learn their origins; you'll find them fascinating. Don't be lazy in the study of your own language.

*Language is the tool with which
you fashion your relationships
and your economic future.*

3. Read Your Audience.

If your audience is a child, search the face of the child so that you know how to proceed. If you don't read your audience, you'll step in the wrong direction. If you miss reading your audience you might get tough when it's time to back off. I was speaking with Zig Ziglar one day to ten thousand people, and Zig told me I had to read the audience. He said, "If ten thousand people turn on you, you're in trouble!" When I first started lecturing I was so consumed with my material and my notes that it took me while to look up from my notes and see how my audience was reacting.

In reading your audience, read first what you can see, such as body language. If your audience have folded arms, if they have frowns on their faces and their chins tucked down, you'll have your work cut out. If people are checking watches or looking at the door, you have to wind up, you can't take much longer.

Then read what you hear. To be a good communicator you have to be a good listener. Listen to questions, the nuances in voices, and the sense of emotion. By listening you can find out if you have to change the direction or the forcefulness of what you are saying.

Finally read what you feel. Pick up emotions in your audience, because if you don't you might do more harm than good by keeping on with your talk. Women are good at this; they pick up the sense or the mood when nothing has been said or done. Men can learn it too, even if they have to try harder. When I was hiring people in the early days of my company, I would always have a woman sit in on the interview. I could pick up what I saw or heard, but I would always turn to the woman to ask, "How did you feel?" I would always take it into account. I didn't always act on it, but I always took that sensitivity into account.

4. Be Intense.

Intensity is the emotional content of communication. This makes your conversation powerful - words loaded with emotion. Express courage, passion, commitment, love and hate in the intensity of your delivery. The emotion can totally change the impact of your words.

If I threw a shirt pin at you, you would feel it prick you. If I fixed the pin to the end of an iron bar and then hurled it at you, I could drive it through your heart. Such is the power of emotion behind a word. You see this aspect of good communication in film and on the stage - the mixture of script and spirit. This is what stirs us and makes a sterling performance.

Your emotions must be well measured. Don't use too much emotion for a minor point. Don't use a canon on a rabbit! You don't need that much firepower. Have you ever heard kids complain about adults making a big deal out of nothing, out of a little deal? As a sophisticated parent, avoid doing that. It is ridiculous. Save your big deal for a big deal. Mr. Shoaff said, "Be generous with a tip, but don't be ridiculous. $5 not $500." Don't go over the top with your emotion.

For a major point though, you have to reach down deep inside yourself and give it all you've got, be generous with your emotion. Sometimes you will need to put both love and hate in the same sentence. A parent can say, "I love you but I hate what you're doing." These days kids need to know that. You've got to love success and hate failure, love health and hate illness, love good and hate evil. Don't be afraid to express these extremes in emotions and not just vocabulary. Keep your intensity near the surface so that it is useable in an instant and so that you can communicate exactly what you mean.

My personal goal is to become a more effective communicator. If you have the same goal, and set about having something good to say and learn how to say it well with intensity to an audience that you can read, you will have extraordinary results.

 Have something good to say
and say it well.

5. Identify With Your Audience.

Build a bridge of awareness and understanding between yourself and your listener. That's easy if the other person is like you, but a little harder if they are not. Females and males, the rich and the poor, the adult and the child, have their work cut out in trying to relate, to identify with each other. As an adult trying to communicate with a child, at least you can go back to your own childhood and find something that you can relate to. Remember especially the emotional impact of those experiences.

6. Tools Of Last Resort.

These are aspects of communication which you can turn to in the last, but not the first, resort. Better if you don't have to use them, but sometimes you can't avoid it.

i. A direct attack.

An indirect approach is better than confrontation. Tell a story about a person who is absent, from which the person who is present can learn from. Third party approach gets better results. But sometimes confrontation is necessary. Remember it can be helpful, but it can also be destructive.

ii. Scolding.

This is very serious, it implies so much. Make sure the

occasion really calls for it. With children, if they have been scolded every day, all day, they end up with scars on the heart. Scolding words can cut deep. Don't take a hatchet to the heart, which is too delicate. Remember that you are wanting to handle the problem without destroying the person's dignity. This may require a delicate operation. If you must scold, make sure it is absolutely necessary.

iii. Sarcasm.

This may be a useful tool, but it is too blunt for most circumstances. Constant sarcasm is not pleasant to be around.

iv. Profanity.

Used sparingly, it may be effective. But if you curse all the time, people will switch off, as with the mother who incessantly yells at her kids. The person who never swears will command instant notice if he or she suddenly uses a profanity to get a point across.

Finally, on the subject of good communication, I want to look at:

The Art of Persuasion.

In sales training we teach there is a difference between presentation and persuasion. It was said of the great orators of antiquity, Cicero and Demosthenes, that when Cicero spoke everybody said, "What a great speech." But when Demosthenes spoke, they said, "Let us march!" That's the difference between presentation and persuasion.

To master the art of persuasion become a good storyteller.

You'll need to collect stories - about people of all ages and backgrounds so that you have stories for every situation. Often the best way to get a point across is to tell a story. A story can expand and illuminate. Jesus was a master storyteller. He said, "The kingdom of heaven is like..." The concept of the kingdom of heaven is beyond imagination but we can relate to what it is like in a story.

Learn to tell your own story.

Use something you've been through, how you've felt, what happened to you, to illustrate a point. Reach back into your past and use your own experience. Sometimes after tragic experiences it takes time before people can speak of it. Many survivors of the holocaust could not speak of their stories and what they saw and experienced for many, many years, but their stories are so important for us.

Have accurate facts.

Make sure a story is really true if that is the claim you are making. You can tell a "suppose so" story - introduce it with "Here's someone," or "Suppose someone..." The truth needs no embellishment. You never know when someone will check the facts of your story.

People ask me if Mr. Shoaff was real, and if the stories I have told about him are true. Why? Because they have been told stories that aren't true. Don't exaggerate the emotion or the facts of a story. Exaggeration is a childish attempt to make up for the lack of self confidence. We exaggerate if we feel ourselves inadequate. Don't do it, because the truth will catch up with you and you don't need the bad feeling anyway. In court, exaggeration throws the entire testimony into doubt. By exaggeration you endanger your whole presentation. What will people know to believe?

Use and acknowledge quotes.

Borrow quotes from everywhere. I use the Bible and the Beatles' song lyrics, and the addresses of Winston Churchill. I find so many quotes that say precisely what I want to say, and I am happy to use what others have said so well.

But don't always borrow other people's words. You have to practise putting things into your own words. Use every opportunity because there are times when actions are no substitute for words. Men might find it more of a challenge to put things into words. Men often rely on flowers but flowers have a limited vocabulary. They don't talk like you do! Flowers can only say, "I remembered." They can't say, "You do incredible things to me! Nobody in this world affects me like you do." When the flowers have died, the card with your words is still kept and remembered. Take birthdays, anniversaries and any other chance to practise using your own words.

Use straight talk.

Tell it like it is and don't cloud the issue. Make it straight, clear and plain. Don't beat around the bush. Sometimes the truth creates a trauma - in my case, giving up my list of blame as to why I didn't have the joy, the self esteem and the money at age twenty-five led to withdrawal symptoms - but people need you to tell them the truth. Mr. Shoaff was direct. He leveled with me. I was fortunate to meet someone who didn't hesitate to talk straight to me after he got to know me, and that straight talk turned my world around. Don't leave people to wander around in the dark; let them know what the deal really is.

Offer solutions.

Talk is not enough, you have to have some answers. Don't leave your talk with an employee, a child, a colleague or a group, in the past with what has happened and what has gone wrong or been done in error. Take your audience into the future - and with language, show them possibilities, the potential, the solutions.

Put out a challenge.

We all respond to a challenge. Part of Mr. Shoaff's challenge was the vision of what I could become. He used to say, "I can see you, Mr. Rohn, as you can be." Try to describe to others the better person they could become. They may not be able to see themselves as better in the future, but you can teach them to look to the future and to the people they can become. Children, especially, need to see themselves as better than they are. As a parent you should help them to get that vision. That is a wonderful challenge.

The best challenge you can give out is in the words, "Let's go and do it!" "Let's..." is so very powerful. The language of antiquity states that, "if two or three will agree on a common purpose nothing will be impossible". The truth is that two or three can dominate an industry; when both parents are united, they make a formidable team. Two does more than double the power of the commitment and dedication of one. It can multiply the force by ten! It doesn't take a million people to create something of value to influence society or industry. Conquering the world is a pretty big job if you try it all on your own, but partnerships, responding to the call "Let's go do it!" can change everything.

Personally, all my businesses are partnerships comprising, at the most, five persons. I have learned the strength of partnerships, and I value it. Of course, partnerships can be tricky, like marriage, but that doesn't mean they can't be a powerful force for success.

Have a passionate belief.
You may not need to work your belief into your presentation but you should have something in life that

stirs you inside. The story of Saul of Tarsus in the New Testament tells of a man who was passionate about grinding Christians into the ground, and then he was converted on the road to Damascus. He translated that immense passion to work for God and became a great Christian leader.

Let the passion in you affect every aspect of your communication. Let it serve you well in the art of persuasion.

USE YOUR
TIME
EFFECTIVELY

CHAPTER FIVE

THE MANAGEMENT OF TIME

The first point I would like to make on time management is that your time is your own, to use how you wish. Your life is your life, and you don't have to let anybody make you in their mould. Success is not money or style, but the progressive realisation of your own goals. You don't have to be like anybody else or act like anybody else, but just shape your dreams and see if you can realise them. If a man has a dream of heading for the hills, living off the land and feeding the squirrels, and that is the dream he achieves, then, in my opinion he is an outstanding success.

One approach to time management is to ignore it altogether! Frankly, I have more respect for the person who decides just to go with the flow and let what happens happen, than for the one who keeps making promises to himself which he doesn't keep.

Remember, it may be perfectly valid to step down t o

something easier. Sometimes you are in a tight spot and you can always say, I don't need this now." A salesman might go into management and find his hours are doubled and his pay is halved. It makes sense for him to go back into sales! That's valid. There is a story about a little girl who says she never gets to see her daddy, he doesn't have time to play. Her daddy is always bringing work home, and her mummy says, "Dear, that's because there's so much he has to do and he can't finish it at the office." The little girls asks, "Why don't they put him in a slower group?" It might be a funny story but it's not a bad idea. Think of your kids. If you are sacrificing too much time with family and friends and children, it might be a good idea to think of a slower group! Some of the things I went for when I was younger cost too much in that regard - if I had known ahead of time what it would cost, I never would have paid.

Another approach to the management of time is to work longer and harder. Give this careful consideration, however, because you can "max out". I went for this in that first year when I couldn't sleep, and my health suffered. I lost 18-20 lbs and I had been skinny to begin with! I went too fast. I used to say, "If ten hours won't do it, I'll do sixteen." I had health challenges at the end of that year and realised that it would be stupid to get rich but be too sick to enjoy it. Of course you have to work hard, but there is a point where you can't work harder.

Sometimes you can't work harder without "maxing out", but remember it's not the hours you put in, but what you put in the hours. You can always work smarter.

This is another approach to the management of time

to get more from yourself. Work smarter. Make yourself more valuable in the same time. To do this there are some essentials you need to do to manage your time effectively.

Time Management Essentials

1. A written set of goals.

When Mr. Shoaff met me he asked to see my current list of goals. He thought he could offer me some help from his experience. I had to say I didn't have a list. He replied that if I didn't have a set of goals, he could guess my bank balance. That was revolutionary to me.

Human beings can set goals, no other animal has that ability, to reach into the future and shape it. Give serious thought to setting goals for your future. You have the ability to dramatically affect your financial future, so why wouldn't you make the effort?

We humans are affected by five things: the environment - whether physical, social or political; events - in our family, community, nation or the world; the results we have achieved or failed to achieve; knowledge; and dreams. We can't disregard the environment, events make up our lives, results reward us with assets or liabilities, knowledge is wealth but dreams shape our future.

Have dreams.

An ancient prophet said that without a vision - a dream, a good clear picture of the future - the people perish. Unless we can see the rewards, the harvest, we aren't motivated to plant or to work. There are two ways to face the future with apprehension, or anticipation. Most people face it with apprehension, and that is because they have left it up to someone else - the government, the church, somebody else. Of course, if you can't see the future, if you can't see, you walk timidly.

To face the future with anticipation, you need to have it in your hand. What sort of health do you want? Envision it. Do you want to be rich? Read the books and envision it. People will do the most extraordinary things if they have strong enough reasons. A reason makes the difference.

My mentor suggested that I was not as far ahead as I wanted to be because I didn't have strong enough reasons - to go to the library, take the class, do the work. If dreams are strong enough they become like magnets; they pull you in their direction. A good fist of goals will not only pull you, it will pull you through. Pull you through bad times and difficulties.

Set goals.

I challenge you to stop now and make a list of all your life's goals. Take as much time as you need. It's fascinating to start pondering what you really want. What would make your life unique, exciting, productive? List everything that you want to do, to achieve. Then go through it and mark the ones you can achieve in one year. Then mark the ones that will take three years. Then mark those that you see as five year goals, and finally any that are ten years in the future.

If you do not have any ten year goals, you need to extend your thinking. You are thinking too short-term. I used to draw a line at ten - I couldn't see past it, but I now understand the power of long term goals. My parents took out a mortgage when they were in their seventies - that was forward thinking. Okay, they paid it off quickly but they had plans for the future. My father has so many goals, things he wants to accomplish, it keeps him alive.

The early astronauts had psychological problems when they got back from their journeys into space, to the moon. Some took to drinking. Why? Because whatever do you do after you've been to the moon? The space programme discovered that the astronauts needed goals to come back to. You need to have something that's ten, or fifteen, or twenty years ahead to keep you going.

Now, I ask you to go through your one year goals and pick out the five most important. This is prioritising your goals. Ask yourself, "Why? What is so important about them?" Write a short paragraph about why these goals are your first priority. Articulate your reasons because this is almost magical in its effect. When the why gets strong, the how gets easy. Many people get lost in the how of getting success. They need to focus more on the why, which makes the how so much easier.

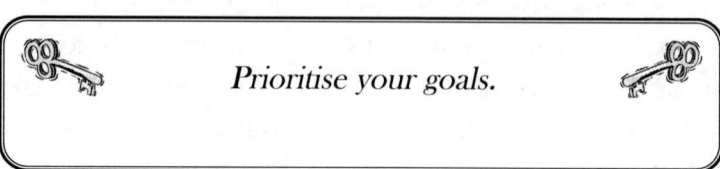

Prioritise your goals.

Consider the man who asks a colleague to recruit twelve husband and wife teams for a business conference the next day. His friend replies that he isn't a salesman or a recruiter - he can't do it. But if the first man offers his colleague $25,000, the effect is magical! Suddenly the friend doesn't even need a training class on recruiting he can go out and do it because the reason is big enough, strong enough.

Purpose is stronger than object.

Your goal may be to have a million dollar home. But ask yourself, "What for?" It's the "what for" that will pull you and pull you through. You may want the home to be the centre of all your family's life, for friends and guests to enjoy. This is your purpose; the home is the object.

Ask yourself, "What kind of person must I become to achieve all I want?" Write another short paragraph in answering this question. This philosophy can be life-changing.

What is the major purpose in setting goals? To entice you to become the person it takes to achieve them. This is the greatest value in life. Mr. Shoaff had me set the goal of becoming a millionaire - why? For what it would make of me to achieve it! For the classes I'd have to take, and the skills I'd have to acquire, and the knowledge and the philosophy I'd have to develop. What was important was not the money, but what I would become.

Set the kind of goals that will make something of you. If you set them too low, so that you don't have to read or take classes or learn anything, you won't grow. Don't join the easy crowd. Go where the demands, the expectations are high. In my circle, the expectations are colossal. Why? For the chance to live at the summit. To live at the summit, the skills, the commitments and dedications are incredible, and that is what is important.

"Strive for perfection," the prophet said. Of course, you can't have perfection in health or marriage or friendship or business, but the key is in the striving. Wherever you arrive when it is finished for you, as long as you have striven to reach perfection, you have made yourself a good, a flourishing life.

Beware. Don't sell out. Don't set goals that will require you to sacrifice friendships, or violate your integrity, or compromise on your virtue or your value. Reach, yes. Stretch, yes. But don't sell out. Remember, Judas got his money, but when he had the fortune in his hands, he was not happy. He was unhappy with himself. The greatest source of unhappiness is in the self. It's not from outside, but from within. And this unhappiness begins so subtly with doing a little less than you could, and letting yourself off the hook. That's where you begin to feel unhappy with yourself. It's the start of the slippery slope. Everyone must suffer one or two pains. The pain of discipline or the pain of regret. My advise is, don't trade the discipline for regret. Discipline weighs ounces, regret weighs pounds. Beware of what you become in pursuit of what you want.

One ancient script asks the question, "What if you gained the whole world and it cost you your soul?" Would that be worth it? No. Some trades in life just aren't worth it. There is the story in Genesis of a first-born twin brother who sold his birthright for a bowl of soup. What a worthless trade!

 Keep your values and don't sell out.

2. Constant review.

Go over your goals regularly and, if necessary, make another list and another until you get it right.

3. Priorities.

Don't spend a lot of effort on something that doesn't yield much equity.

4. A written set of plans.

Essential to time management, is having a game plan. You may need a wall planner, or whiteboard to set this out. If you also use a calendar, make sure you have projects and your other calendar appointments side by side on the planner. Your projects will include advertising, recruiting, training, but you may be in the habit of putting your family on the calendar. Add the family commitments to the game plan. If you can show your children that they rate space up there with your business projects they love it. It also makes it easier for you to see where projects and family time may clash, and you may need to renegotiate with the family beforehand.

Put everything on the game plan. If any project becomes too much and overloads the sheet, take it off and give it its own game plan. Game plans may run over one, two, or three years. You may not be doing business around the world, or running great finance or property projects, but everyone benefits when their projects are set out visually like this.

5. Learn to separate major from minor.

For example, a minor conversation may be pleasantries and not much more. A major conversation requires more time. Time in the presence of the prospect. Minor time is getting to the prospect, planning the prospect time, doing the work book.

6. Don't mistake movement for achievement.

You can go, go, go without getting to your goal. You can be very busy going nowhere or going in circles.

7. Concentration.

I used to try to start my business day in the shower - not a good idea. In the shower enjoy the shower. At breakfast enjoy your breakfast, don't have your mind elsewhere. "Wherever you are, be there," is a title from Readers' Digest. Give your project, and people the gift of attention. This is especially powerful with children. Don't be distracted when talking to them. Nelson Rockefeller held a news conference in my town once and I made a point of stepping up to him and telling him my name. He repeated my name and asked if I lived there in Idaho. He looked right at me and shook my hand and said, "I'm always happy to come to Idaho." He gave me the gift of attention and I remember the details of that to this day. Give this gift to your workmates, your customers, your children. Preoccupation is a danger.

8. Learn to say no.

This is essential. Learn to say no to activities and to people. If you would be a serious leader, you need to ask yourself the following questions: Who am I around? What are they doing to me - what have they got me reading where have they got me going, how have they got me talking? What have they got me becoming? Is it okay?

If it is not okay, then you need to start saying no to those people who are influencing you. Mr. Shoaff gave me this phrase - "Never mistake the power of influence." Influence is powerful and subtle. We wouldn't let someone drive us off course but we might let them nudge us off course. The next thing we know, we're way over there and we don't know how we got there. We just felt a little elbow!

There will be times when you need to disassociate. Separate yourself from the wrong influence. If it comes down to the wire, you may have to do this but don't do it frivolously. If you have to be polite, say, "No, thank you." If you don't have to be polite, just say, "No."

Direction determines destination. Not to think so is naive. If you have to change tracks, better early than late.

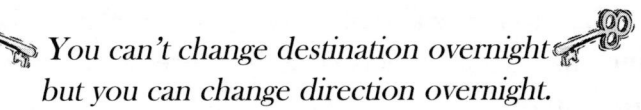

You can't change destination overnight but you can change direction overnight.

Sometimes you can work out a limited association. Some people you can be with for an hour or so, but not a few days; some you might associate with for a day or two, but not for years. Limit your association where necessary, to make sure you keep on track.

And there are people with whom you will want to expand your association. Find the people whom you want to be around. Spend more time with them. If the people aren't available, spend time with their books and tapes and get yourself some good influence that is going to help your health and relationships and economic situation.

9. When you work, work; when you play, play.

Don't mix the two. Work is too important to play. Make a work day a work day, and a play day, a play day. Try not to mix them on the same day. If you are going to knock off early to play, there's a good chance it will influence the work you do earlier in the day. Don't play at work it's too serious. Your future depends on it, your family depends on it. To play around at work shows an unsophisticated intelligence. Too much is at stake. Avoid at all costs the reputation that you play at work.

And don't work at play. When you are at the beach, don't have your mind back at the office. It's not good for your family.

Don't play unless you deserve it. Don't have a party unless you deserve it, it doesn't taste good. The ancient prophet said it tastes bitter in the mouth. In my circle, we work hard and play hard, and it feels good.

10. Analyse yourself.

Ask yourself, "When am I at my best?" Some people are night people, others are better first thing in the morning. Work out when you get your best work done. This may change throughout your life. I used to be running at midnight, but now I love to watch the sun come up.

11. Have a look at your habits.

Experience has shown me that I am a poor courier - my company used to give me cheques or documents to deliver when I was travelling, but the cheques would still be in my pocket when the suit went to the dry cleaner's! Finally the word went out - "Don't give the chairman anything to deliver!" Perhaps you are not good at figures and have troubling balancing your cheque book; get somebody to do it for you. Find out where you are weak and organise a way to cover for that.

12. You need to consider your telephone skills, too.

Make an agenda before you make an important call, don't leave it to your memory. If you forget important points, you won't look good. Be efficient; this is especially important in long distance calls. Also, if you have a written record of your agenda you can refer to it later if there is some query over what was covered in the call. This could prove so important.

If you are doing work at home, don't let the telephone at home intrude. Let it serve. Remember every advantage has its danger. When you have family time, you should shut the world down. Even the important calls can wait because family time is most important. Consider putting in a second phone line if your home phone is in demand.

13. Develop a hassle list.

Make a list of all the things that bug you - and then see how many things you can take off that list with the least amount of cost. You'll be surprised how little it costs to get some of the hassles out of your life. Consider the man who hates mowing the lawn and gets out of breath and ends up cussing, but won't part with a little cash to pay the neighbourhood kid to do it. Is it worth the heart attack? It seems to me that the neighbourhood kid needs all the encouragement he can get in his enterprise.

14. Read the good books on time management.

Read Bliss, Mackay, Laken and others like them.

15. Become more alert to antiquated systems.

Things are changing so fast, there is sure to be a new and better and faster way to do something that is hassling you.

16. Learn to ask questions up front.

Sometimes we talk for an hour and then ask a question of the person we are talking to which could have saved us fifty-five minutes. We can jump to wrong conclusions, and address issues which are not the primary ones, when a question, or series of questions could have revealed the real problem. Say, for example, a salesman's figures are down. He's showing up late and not putting in so much effort. Instead of giving him a talk on activity, a simple question could go straight to the cause? "How come a good salesman like you is making hard work of things, John?" Personal problems may be at the bottom of it, and John may well say, with relief, "I thought no one would ever ask." In such situations, one question may not be enough: two or three may get you through to the point where enough trust is established to bring the issue to the surface.

17. Learn to think on paper.

Keep a journal. Now, a picture is worth a thousand

words and our lives can be recorded in a series of little clicks to leave for our children and grandchildren and future generations; but a record of your life in words is immensely valuable too. Keep notes of ideas, and pointers you pick up in books, from sermons and poems and films. Keep your notes in a proper bound journal, not on lots of loose pieces of paper. If you don't have your journal with you when you need to record something, make a note and transfer it later. Personally, I love to have expensive journals to reflect something of the value of what I record in them. If you are in a congregation or audience and you are the only one taking notes, it may look weird, but it shows how serious you are to learn.

A project book is another invaluable tool. Keep a running account of all your projects in a loose leaf folder marked out with colour-coded tabs. When a project finishes, take the tab and the pages out and make room for new ones. You can also keep a running account on your business contacts and the people who work for you.

Maintain a 'To Do' list. A daily schedule of all the things you want to accomplish for the day, whom you want to meet, what calls you have to make, written out on paper. You can buy prepared pages for your diary in any newsagent. With a 'To Do' list, a project book and a journal you can do business out of your briefcase.

These are all just small tips on time management, but sometimes small tips can make a huge difference.

- *Jim Rohn*

THE FORMULA
FOR
FINANCIAL SUCCESS

CHAPTER SIX

FINANCIAL INDEPENDENCE

For the last thirty years I have been talking to teenagers on how to be rich by age forty. When I was younger I wasn't really sure what being rich was, and in my talks I could see the children struggling to come up with a picture of rich for themselves. Then I decided to call it wealth, but I found that both these words can be a little overwhelming.

There are two questions to ask concerning being rich or wealthy. Is it okay to be rich? Is it okay to strive for it?

Some folk think you have to step on people and compromise yourself or become greedy to become wealthy, but I have come to other conclusions.

I like to consider these questions: If you could do better, should you?

This has a moral and spiritual aspect, sure, but it is also practical. If you could do better, should you? Or should you pray instead? I believe in prayer, but I also believe in labour. It seems to me, from Scripture, that 6/7ths of our lives is to be devoted to enterprise. Now, if you could get good enough at your labour to make a fortune, is it okay to amass that fortune?

I used to think that poverty was a virtue and that we all should embrace it. But I discovered that poverty was a curse. It seems to me that Jesus didn't direct us to be poor, but to be so wealthy we could help the poor. Now, I'm no theologian, but that is how I see it. So I just ask the question to myself, "If I could do better, should I?"

With a normal income and a normal working life, i.e. it is possible to become financially independent. Financially independent is how I now describe being rich or wealthy. To define financial independence I say it is the ability to live from the income of your own resources. Some people might be happy with a modest income, others need millions. That is not the issue. The question is, if you could manage to do that, in a normal working life without stepping on anybody or sacrificing your virtue, would you go for it? I maintain that if you start at age fifteen you can be financially independent at age forty-five.

How?

First, you need a good philosophy. The philosophy of the poor is to spend the money and invest what is left. They would swear to you that there is nothing left, therefore they can't invest. Rich people invest their money and spend what is left. What a difference. It's not the amount that makes the difference, it's the philosophy. When Mr. Shoaff said, "Set a goal to become a millionaire," I thought that could hardly be possible. But I found out it was fairly simple. Everybody has the money. Poor people have the money to spend on self-development books.

Even a forty dollar book is only fifteen doughnuts!

It's not the money,
but how it is allocated,
how it is spent.

I was once challenged by a lady who told me I shouldn't go around preaching financial independence to young people. She said I was holding out false hope, because young couples today need all they could earn just to get by. I challenged her to think of a young couple she knew who together were making about $2500 a month. I asked, "How much do you think they would say it takes to keep the wolf from the door. Would it be $2500 a month?" She agreed that was so. I then challenged her to think of another couple who earned $3000 a month. I asked, "What amount would they say they needed just to get by?" She agreed they would say, "All of it." So what happened to the extra money? It disappeared through errors of judgement and philosophy. If the second couple learned to live as the first couple, and invested the extra $500, they would, in twenty years, be financially independent. They do not have to move countries - they just have to reallocate resources.

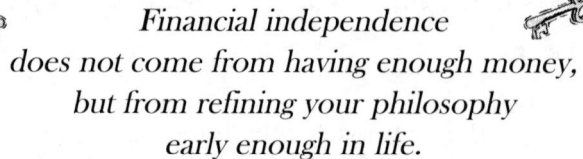

*Financial independence
does not come from having enough money,
but from refining your philosophy
early enough in life.*

You also need to reallocate your resources - both time and money - if you wish to be financially independent. When you learn to do this, your life can dramatically change. I was in a hurry and wanted to do it fast so I worked extra hard on that. First, I increased my income by becoming more valuable in the market place and then I developed a strategy for putting it to work.

Ask yourself, "Where are my present allocations of resources, and my disciplines taking me?" Look one, three, five, ten years ahead. Are they taking you where you want to go? Celebrate if the answer is yes! But if the answer is no, then let's fix it.

My strategy for financial independence can begin with a dollar. I teach teenagers in my seminars to never spend more than seventy cents. When Mr. Shoaff found me I was busy spending one hundred and ten cents! He told me I had to put together a financial statement. He called it a picture of where I was financially at the time. He showed me how to subtract liabilities from assets to discover my net financial worth I protested that it wouldn't look very good, but he insisted that the importance wasn't in how it looked, but in my doing it. He was right – when I did the exercise I was so embarrassed: I even included my old shoes in my list of assets. It made me see that I had bought the wrong plan. I decided then not to spend more than the seventy cents.

So, what do you do with the other thirty cents? Allot ten cents to charity. I maintain that nothing teaches a child character better than generosity to worthy projects. Allot ten cents for active capital. You live in a capital-istic society, so why shouldn't you have your own capi-tal? Why leave it in the hands of the government or the hands of a few businessmen? This is the money you will use to make a profit, and it is profits that make a fortune, not wages. Wages only make a living. The secret is to not use all your profit. Don't eat your seed corn. Use the last 10 cents as passive capital. Invest it for interest, and let the interest compound. If children start on this simple programme early, and pursue it for fifteen or twenty years, they can be financially independent before they are middle aged!

If you can't start out sticking strictly to the ratios in this programme, that doesn't matter. Even if you have to use ninety-seven cents, and invest, give and work with the other three cents, you can begin to change. But at least set up the ideal. As long as you have the ideal in front of you and as you progress - increase your skills, become more knowledgeable, you set aside more and more and use less and less you will be improving your net worth I tell you that when you move in my circles you will have so much to invest and so much income coming in from it, it will be embarrassing! You can get to the point where you can live well - like I can - on ten percent of your income.

When you embark on this programme, you must

keep strict accounts. An ancient story tells of a master who was going on a journey and he gave five talents to one servant, two to another and one to another. He required them to do something with their measures of gold. Why was there this difference? Why was one given more than the other? We don't know; that's just the way it was. The important thing is that there were no zeros! The story goes on to say that when the master returned he wanted to know what the servants had done with their talents. The fellow who had five talents had turned it into ten, and was rewarded with a "Well done!" The fellow who had been given two, had managed to turn that into four - it didn't look as good as the ten but at least it was better than what he had started with. Then the master called the servant who had one and asked him what he had done with it. This fellow still only had one. The master's response was to become enraged. He cast the servant out and took the last single talent and gave it to the one who had ten already. The story does not tell us why. We don't know why the master did that. But we do know that it keeps happening! At least, the first fellow would be able to multiply that one talent and use it to take care of the last miserable servant.

There are three things we can learn from this story. First, it is important to at least do what you can. I challenge you to set yourself an "at least" list - of things which you will "at least" achieve between now and the next year. Then, at least, you will be able to hold your head up.

The second point is this: whatever you don't use, you

lose. Whether it's talent, or energy or ability - if you don't use it, you'll lose it. The third thing is that when much is given, much is required. That is why the master required ten as a return on five. Had the first servant only turned the five into six, it would not have been enough.

That is why it is important to keep strict accounts. Remember: if your outgoings exceed your income, your upkeep becomes your downfall!

Finally, if you would be financially independent, have a good look at your attitude. What is your attitude to paying your bills? If you hate paying bills it means you hate increasing your liabilities and increasing your assets. I used to think that everybody hated paying their bills. Then Mr. Shoaff told me, "No." I used to hate paying my taxes, but paying taxes is the way we feed the goose that lays the golden egg. Don't you want someone to stay awake all night while you sleep, in order to maintain your security? Now, sometimes it seems that the goose may well eat too much, but better a fat goose than no goose! Anyway, we all eat too much. Let not one appetite accuse another. Everybody must pay.

Everybody has to pay. There is a story about Jesus watching people putting in their contributions to the Temple treasury. One old woman put in two pennies, and Jesus said this represented more than all the other donations. Note that Jesus did not run after the woman and give her back the two pennies because she was so abysmally poor and that was all she had. He left them there. Why? Because everybody has to pay.

In Conclusion

Leadership is the challenge to be more than mediocre. Society will let you get by being average, but if you want to be better than average, you have to require it of yourself. Leadership is the hope of the future. Somebody had to go out front and turn on the lights.

Refinement of leadership requires that you:

◆ Be strong but not rude.

◆ Be kind but not weak

◆ Be bold but not a bully.

◆ Be thoughtful but not lazy.

◆ Be humble but not timid.

◆ Be proud but not arrogant.

◆ Use humour but not folly.

◆ Work with people who deserve it, not the people who need it.

◆ Show people how to deserve it.

◆ Reward people for small steps of progress.

◆ See people as they are and share with them what you see.

- See people better than they are and see things that don't yet exist.

- Have faith.

- Let your people borrow your vision until they can see for themselves.

Finally, all leaders must understand the fact of good and evil. I can't stress this too strongly. Evil is a very real danger. You must understand the story of the frog and the scorpion. It goes like this:

A frog and a scorpion arrived at the river at about the same time and the frog was about to jump in and swim to the other side. The scorpion stopped him and explained that he couldn't swim. He asked the frog to carry him across. The frog said, "No. You'll sting me." The scorpion said, "Of course, I wouldn't! It would make me drown too." And so the frog said, "Yes." Sure enough, half way across the river, the scorpion stung the frog. Why? Because he was a scorpion.

You can't afford the productivity of some people. But you can't always avoid them. Even Jesus had his challenges - he took Judas on board. But as a leader you must both be like a mother and a guard. Be ever vigilant. Have a trowel in one hand and a sword in the other as you build your city wall.

Today I am a wealthy man because of my heritage. By virtue of place and time I fell heir to systems and knowledge that I never paid for. This was my heritage.

I am also a wealthy man because of my experiences-they are my coins and currency.

I am wealthy because of my knowledge which is power.

I am wealthy because of my future in which my dreams can be actualised.

I am wealthy because of my friends. Make sure you make the kind of friends on your way up that will take you in on the way down!

Finally, I am wealthy because of love. In the end it is better to live in a tent with someone you love than in a mansion on your own. The greatest gift is love. The price tag on that is immeasurable.

 *Let others live small lives but not you.*

This is my challenge to you. By reading this book you are already putting yourself in the top five percent. I love motivating people like you. It is an investment for me. Let others cry over small hurts, and argue over non-essentials, but not you.

I challenge you to go on from here and help people with their lives, not just their jobs. People need life skills, a life plan, not just a game plan for money.

There is an ancient promise that if you work on your gifts they will make a place for you. Many years ago I got very serious about working on my gifts and look now where they have taken me. I'm asking you to work on your gifts, and you will get invitations to places you never dreamed about, places that will awe you.

Ask for God's help but never make it an excuse for inactivity. There was a story about the man who turned a rock pile into a beautiful garden and a passerby congratulated him. "You and the good Lord have done a great job here." The man replied, "I can buy that. But you should have seen this place a few years ago when God had it all by himself."

You are surrounded by talent and skill and literature and music. You are surrounded by opportunity and possibilities. Take a little from this book and put it to work so that folk will say of the people whom you would lead - your children, your students, your employees - "they're in good hands."